# MARTIN LUTHER KING JR.

## GREAT LIVES IN GRAPHICS

Button
BOOKS

When **Martin Luther King Jr** was growing up in America the city he lived in was segregated, which meant that children with "coloured" skin couldn't use the same parks, schools, restaurants or shops as those with white skin. This made Martin sad and he vowed that one day he would "turn this world upside down". He worked hard to become good at speaking in public and when, years later, he was given the chance to stand up and say what he thought about the way black people were treated in America, he gave a speech that has gone down in history as the greatest of all time.

"I have a dream," he said, "that my four little children will one day live in a nation where they will not be judged by the colour of their skin but by the content of their character." His powerful words inspired America to end segregation and take steps towards a fairer society. This is Martin's story – it looks at how a young black American overcame the obstacles in front of him and used peaceful protest to change the world.

# MARTIN'S WORLD

## 1929
Martin is born on 15 January in Atlanta, Georgia, USA

## 1931
Empire State Building opens in New York

## 1932
Franklin D Roosevelt elected President

## 1933
Adolf Hitler becomes leader of Germany

## 1934
Donald Duck makes first appearance

## 1936
Jesse Owens wins four golds at Berlin Olympics

## 1937
Boxer Joe Louis is heavyweight champion

## 1939
World War II begins

## 1941
Japan bombs Pearl Harbor. America and Canada join WWII

## 1944
Goes to Morehouse College age 15

## 1947
Jackie Robinson is first black American to play major league baseball

## 1948
Graduates from Morehouse and attends Crozer

## 1951
Graduates from Crozer

## 1952
First Mr Potato Head toy sold

## 1953
Marries aspiring singer Coretta Scott

## 1954
Becomes minister of Dexter Avenue Baptist Church in Montgomery, Alabama

## 1963
Leads boycott of white-owned businesses. Arrested and writes *Letter from a Birmingham Jail* from his cell

Delivers "I Have a Dream" speech at Lincoln Memorial in Washington DC

John F Kennedy assassinated

## 1955
Earns doctorate from Boston University

Leads Montgomery bus boycott

## 1956
Martin's home is bombed

## 1962
Arrested at prayer vigil, spends two weeks in jail

## 1964
*Time* magazine names Martin "Man of the Year" for 1963

Arrested at whites-only restaurant in Florida

Awarded Nobel Peace Prize

## 1957
Asks government to pass Civil Rights Bill to protect black people's right to vote

Appears on cover of *Time* magazine

## 1961
Arrested at protest in Albany

## 1965
Leads peaceful march from Selma to Montgomery demanding voting rights for black Americans

Gives speech against Vietnam War

## 1960
Arrested at sit-in at whites-only lunch counter

John F Kennedy elected President

## 1958
Meets President Dwight D Eisenhower

Stabbed with letter opener at book signing

## 1968
Leads march to support striking sanitation workers

Assassinated at the Lorraine Motel in Memphis, Tennessee

# MIGHTY MARTIN

Martin was close to his family. He grew up in a four-bedroom house in Atlanta, Georgia, one of three children born to Alberta Williams and Martin Luther King Sr – also known as Daddy King. Daddy King was strict and quizzed the children about politics at meal times, while Martin's mum played the piano and filled the house with music. Martin worked hard at home and at school, but he also loved to play pranks . . .

UNITED STATES OF AMERICA

BORN IN ATLANTA, GEORGIA

MIDDLE CHILD

When Martin was born he was named Michael after his dad. When he turned five, his dad changed both their names to "Martin Luther" in honour of a famous religious thinker

## RELIGIOUS

Recited Bible verse
at dinnertime

· · · · · · · · · · · · · · ·

Dad, uncle, grandad and
great-grandad were
all preachers

· · · · · · · · · · · · · · ·

Went to Sunday School

## FUN-LOVING!

Played baseball

Wanted to be
a fireman

Loved Monopoly

## MUSICAL

Mum ran the church choir

Liked to sing

Played piano

## JOKER!

Popped the heads off sister's
dolls to use as baseballs!

Adjusted piano stool so it collapsed
when teacher sat down!

Tied mum's fox fur to a stick
and poked it through bushes
to scare passersby!

## FAIR-MINDED

STOOD UP FOR WHAT WAS RIGHT

SPOKE OUT AGAINST WRONGDOING

TREATED PEOPLE FAIRLY

**DID YOU KNOW?** Martin was a strong student – he skipped two grades and graduated from high school at 15

# BLACK &WHITE

When Martin was three years old, his best friend was a white boy whose dad owned a shop across the street from his home. At six they started school, but they couldn't study together. Martin had to go to a school for black children, and his friend went to one for whites. One day the boy told Martin they couldn't play together anymore because his dad didn't want him playing with a black person. Martin felt bad and ran home to his mum to ask her why. She explained that black and white people were treated differently in America, and that there were unfair rules - called Jim Crow laws - that black people had to follow.

## JIM CROW LAWS

**THERE WILL BE SEPARATE SCHOOLS FOR WHITE AND BLACK CHILDREN. NO BLACK CHILD CAN ATTEND A WHITE SCHOOL, AND NO WHITE CHILD CAN ATTEND A BLACK SCHOOL**

**BLACK AND WHITE PEOPLE ARE NOT TO RIDE IN THE SAME CARS**

**RESTAURANTS SHALL NOT SERVE THE TWO RACES IN THE SAME ROOM**

**THEATRES MUST HAVE SEPARATE ENTRANCES FOR WHITE AND BLACK PEOPLE, AND SEPARATE SEATING AREAS AS WELL**

**IF YOU WANT TO VOTE, YOU MUST FILL OUT A FORM REGARDING YOUR RACIAL HISTORY, AND YOU MUST ALSO PAY A POLL TAX**

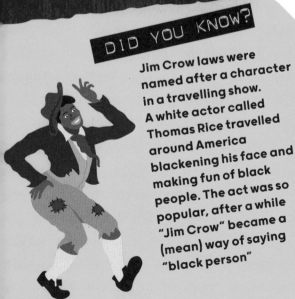

### DID YOU KNOW?

Jim Crow laws were named after a character in a travelling show. A white actor called Thomas Rice travelled around America blackening his face and making fun of black people. The act was so popular, after a while "Jim Crow" became a (mean) way of saying "black person"

THERE WILL BE SEPARATE PARKS FOR BLACK AND WHITE PEOPLE. BLACK PEOPLE CANNOT ENTER A PARK FOR WHITES AND WHITE PEOPLE CANNOT ENTER A PARK FOR BLACKS

BUSES WILL BE SEGREGATED, WITH SEPARATE SECTIONS FOR WHITE PEOPLE AND BLACK PEOPLE

AMUSEMENT PARKS ARE FOR WHITE PEOPLE ONLY

BLACK PEOPLE CANNOT USE PUBLIC SWIMMING POOLS

# SIGNS OF THE TIMES

Signs telling black Americans where they could and couldn't go were everywhere. They were a hurtful reminder to black people that they weren't treated the same as white people

**PARAMOUNT THEATRE**
COLORED ENTRANCE
*Enjoy Good Shows in Comfort*

**IMPERIAL LAUNDRY CO.**
WE WASH FOR WHITE PEOPLE ONLY

WAITING ROOM FOR COLORED ONLY
→
BY ORDER POLICE DEPT.

REST ROOMS
WHITE      COLORED
←      L&N      →

When Martin was 14 he entered a public speaking competition. He wrote a speech about the unfairnes of Jim Crow laws, and travelled to Dublin in Georgic to deliver it. On the bus ride home, the driver asked him to give up his seat to a white passenger. Martir had to stand for two hours. **"It was the angriest I've ever been in my life,"** he said.

WASHINGTON

MONTANA

NORTH DAKOTA

OREGON

IDAHO

WYOMING

SOUTH DAKOTA

NEBRASKA

NEVADA

UTAH

COLORADO

KANSAS

CALIFORNIA

MEMPHIS

1968

**Martin is assassinated**

OKLAHOMA

MARION

1953

**Marries Coretta at her family home**

ARIZONA

NEW MEXICO

TEXAS

# A WORLD OF DIFFERENCE

When Martin grew up his dad was a Baptist minister at the local church and Martin's family had enough money, but life was hard because of segregation (the system that kept black and white people separate). Listening to his dad give sermons, Martin learned how powerful words could be at helping others to understand ideas. He decided he would become a minister like his dad and use words to change people's minds about the Jim Crow laws and the way black people were treated in America.

MINNESOTA

WISCONSIN

MICHIGAN

IOWA

ILLINOIS

INDIANA

OHIO

MISSOURI

KENTUCKY

TENNESSEE

ARKANSAS

MISSISSIPPI

LOUISIANA

ALABAMA

GEORGIA

FLORIDA

NORTH CAROLINA

SOUTH CAROLINA

VIRGINIA

PENNSYLVANIA

NEW YORK

NEW HAMPSHIRE
VERMONT

MAINE

MASSACHUSETTS
RHODE ISLAND
CONNECTICUT

NEW JERSEY
MARYLAND
DELAWARE

**BOSTON**

**1952**
Meets Coretta Scott and falls in love

**1955**
PhD from Boston University – now called Dr King

**CHESTER**

**1951**
Graduates from Crozer

**WASHINGTON DC**

**1958**
Meets President Eisenhower

**1963**
Gives "I have a dream" speech

**ATLANTA**

**1929**
Martin is born

**1944**
Goes to Morehouse College at just 15

**MONTGOMERY**

**1955**
Bus boycott starts

**BIRMINGHAM**

**1963**
Writes *Letter from a Birmingham Jail*

# NORTH VS SOUTH

Jim Crow laws were based largely in America's southern states. After the Civil War in 1865 slavery was abolished, but the southern states passed Jim Crow laws to make sure black people found life hard and would continue to work on their farms.

# HAPPY FAMILIES!

When Martin was 22 he travelled to Boston to begin studying for his PhD. A friend gave him the phone number of a music student named Coretta Scott, and the two met for lunch. Before they'd even finished their meal, Martin said his mind was made up. "We ought to get married someday," he told Coretta. Luckily for Martin Coretta agreed, and two years later, they did.

## MARTIN LUTHER KING JR
(1929-1968)

### MARRIED 1953

## WIFE
### Coretta Scott King
(1927-2006)

When Martin and Coretta married, hotels wouldn't rent rooms to black people, so they spent their wedding night in a friend's funeral parlour!

### DAUGHTER
Yolanda Denise King
(1955-2007)

### SON
Martin Luther King III
(1957-present)

### SON
Dexter Scott King
(1961-present)

### DAUGHTER
Bernice Albertine King
(1963-present)

When Yolanda was six years old she asked her dad if he would take her to Funtown, a local amusement park. Martin was sad because he had to tell her Funtown was segregated, and black people weren't allowed to go. "Daddy's working on it," he said.

## FATHER
### Martin Luther King Sr
(1899-1984)

## MOTHER
### Alberta Williams King
(1904-1974)

Martin's mum taught him that although he had to follow the Jim Crow laws, that didn't mean they were right.

**"You are as good as anyone,"**

she told Martin.

Daddy King never accepted the Jim Crow laws. When Martin was young Daddy King took him to buy some shoes. They entered the shop and sat down, but the clerk asked them to move to the "coloured" section at the back. Daddy King refused and stormed out.

## SISTER
### Christine King Farris
(1927-present)

## BROTHER
### Alfred Daniel Williams King
(1930-1969)

# NEXT GENERATION!

Today Martin's grandchild Yolanda Renee King is carrying on his good work. At the age of nine she made a surprise appearance at a march against guns in Washington, saying: "My grandfather had a dream that his four little children would not be judged by the colour of their skin, but the content of their character. I have a dream that enough is enough and that this should be a gun-free world, period."

## DID YOU KNOW?

When it was time to wash the dishes after supper, Martin's sister Christine remembers that Martin would suddenly need to use the bathroom!

The meeting to organise the boycott was held at Martin's church, where he was a minister. They formed a group called the Montgomery Improvement Association (MIA) and asked Martin to be their leader

To get the word out, they stayed up all night making flyers

**40,000** black bus riders boycotted the system the next day

SUPPORT ROSA PARKS DON'T RIDE THE BUSES

# BUS BOYCOTT

CLEVELAND AVE

On 1 December, 1955, a black woman named Rosa Parks sat on the bus on her way home from work in Montgomery, Alabama. She was seated in the front row of the "coloured" section. The bus was busy and when the white seats were filled the bus driver asked Rosa to give up her seat for a white passenger. Rosa said: "I had given up my seat before, but this day, I was especially tired. Tired from my work as a seamstress. Tired from the ache in my heart." Rosa refused, and she was arrested. When local civil rights leaders found out they were angry. They got together and organised a boycott – they asked black people not to use the buses until the laws were changed to make them fair.

2857

**ROSA PARKS**

Rosa had met the driver who asked her to give up her seat before. A few years earlier, she had paid her fare at the front of the bus then stepped off so she could re-enter through the back door. The driver had pulled away before she could get back on the bus. This was a mean trick that some white drivers played on black people.

# INSTEAD...

- People shared cars
- 200 volunteers offered the use of their cars
- 100 pick-up stations were established
- Black taxi drivers charged just 10 cents for a ride **10c**
- Black churches donated shoes as people wore theirs out walking
- People rode bicycles, some even rode mules

**— 90%** of black passengers didn't ride the bus

# WHITES FIGHT BACK

- Some white people got angry and tried to stop the boycott
- Martin was arrested and fined $500
- 25 nasty telephone calls a day to Martin's home
- Local insurers stopped insuring cars used in the boycott
- Boycotters were fired from their jobs
- Martin's home was firebombed

**2857**

# 381 DAYS
The boycott lasted for over a year

# DEC 21 1956

Finally, the US Supreme Court ruled that segregation on buses was illegal. The next day, Martin waited at the bus stop in front of his house. When the bus arrived, he got on and sat down at the front. The boycott had worked!

The boycott was in lots of newspapers across America, and Martin became known as a leader and activist for civil rights (the rights that everyone has to be treated equally).

# PEOPLE POWER!

Martin believed in peaceful protest. While he was at college he read about Indian leader Mahatma Gandhi and the non-violent actions he used to make the British government listen and give India independence. Martin saw that more people were likely to support the black community's cause if they protested peacefully and he encouraged those in the civil rights movement to "meet hate with love", even when they themselves were met with violence.

## WHY PROTEST?

We have a system of government called a democracy, which means "ruled by the people". In a democracy, people have a say about how their country is run. Usually they do this by voting, but protesting is another important way for people to get their voices heard – especially for the younger generation

## NON-VIOLENT VS VIOLENT

Non-violent protests are **2x** as likely to succeed as violent ones because:

They are much bigger, attracting **4x** as many people as violent protests

People from all different parts of society take part, making them more effective at disrupting everyday life

**DID YOU KNOW?** Martin and Gandhi (right) were both inspired by American philosopher Henry David Thoreau. In 1849 he wrote an essay called "Civil Disobedience" in which he said that people should refuse to obey unjust laws

## MAGIC NUMBER

Historically, once **3.5%** of the population actively engages in a peaceful protest, political change is guaranteed

## PEACEFUL PROTESTS HAPPENING NOW!

Black Lives Matter

Extinction Rebellion

School Strike for Climate

Women's March

## DID YOU KNOW?

Martin's son Dexter described how his family once burned their toy guns in a garden bonfire. "Non-violence wasn't just for marches and protests," he said. "It was for home as well."

## 5 WAYS TO PROTEST PEACEFULLY

**STRIKE**

**BOYCOTT**

**MARCH**

**DEMONSTRATE**

**SIT-IN**

## KNOW YOUR RIGHTS

### FREEDOM OF EXPRESSION AND ASSEMBLY
You have the right to gather with others peacefully and voice your opinion

### FREEDOM FROM EXCESSIVE USE OF FORCE
Police must avoid using force at peaceful protests

### FREEDOM FROM ARBITRARY ARREST AND DETENTION
If police arrest you, they have to tell you why, and you have the right to see a lawyer soon after

### PROTECTION OF RIGHT TO FREEDOM OF ASSEMBLY
Police have to help and not restrict peaceful protests

### RIGHT TO MEDICAL ASSISTANCE
If you are injured you have a right to immediate medical help

### RIGHT TO COMPLAIN
If police violate these rights they must give you information on how you can complain

# JAILBIRD!

After the Montgomery Bus Boycott Martin travelled all over America giving speeches and demonstrating for civil rights, shining a spotlight on racial injustice and inspiring students to hold their own non-violent protests. Some staged "sit-ins", where they sat down at whites-only lunch counters and refused to move until they were served. Others made "freedom rides" on buses to show that segregation was still happening. They were shouted at and beaten but they didn't fight back. Martin marched in Birmingham, Alabama and was arrested. Across the South, white people's businesses began to lose money, while the jails filled up with black Americans.

POLICE DEPT
BIRMINGHAM ALA
118593 412'63

**1,000** black children skipped school to join the Birmingham Children's Crusade and hundreds were arrested. The next day another 1,000 children turned up and the police used dogs and fire hoses to stop them marching. Newspapers printed the pictures and people were shocked

**Daily Post**

### CHILDREN HURT IN RIGHTS MARCH

After his 13th arrest, Martin wrote a Letter from a Birmingham Jail, in which he said non-violent protests were an important way to create change and that "injustice anywhere is a threat to justice everywhere"

# 10 MAY, 1963
## BIRMINGHAM'S LEADERS AGREED TO END SEGREGATION IN THE CITY

OVER THE NEXT 10 WEEKS, MORE THAN

# 750
CIVIL RIGHTS PROTESTS

TOOK PLACE IN

# 186
AMERICAN CITIES

LEADING TO ALMOST

# 15,000
ARRESTS

## HOW THE CIVIL RIGHTS PROTESTS UNFOLDED

**1960** Four black students in Greensboro, North Carolina start the sit-in movement, refusing to leave a whites-only lunch counter

**1961** Black and white "Freedom Riders" ride buses to the South and try to use whites-only restrooms and waiting rooms

**1963** Water cannons and dogs used on protestors at non-violent demonstrations in Birmingham, Alabama

**DID YOU KNOW?**

Between 1957 and 1968 Martin is said to have travelled

**6** MILLION MILES

In that time he made

**2,500** SPEECHES

# "I HAVE A DREAM"

## WASHINGTON DC

MARYLAND

WASHINGTON DC

VIRGINIA

1000M

THE WHITE HOUSE

ELLIPSE

MARCH STARTING POINT

CONSTITUTION AVENUE

CONSTITUTION GARDENS

LINCOLN MEMORIAL

EAST/WEST WALKWAY

WASHINGTON MONUMENT

1 MILE ROUTE

RALLY SITE

WEST POTOMAC PARK

---

More than **2,000** buses

**20** trains

**10** planes

chartered to get marchers to Washington

Black and white people marched hand in hand

On 28 August, 1963 Martin gave his famous "I Have a Dream" speech at a march in Washington DC, the nation's capital. Speaking to a huge crowd of more than a quarter of a million people, he called for an end to Jim Crow laws and equal rights for all Americans.

**5,000** police officers and national guardsmen were ready in case of violence, but the march was peaceful

The March on Washington was the largest ever held in the nation's capital up to that time

"I have a dream that my four little children will one day live in a nation where they will not be judged by the colour of their skin, but by the content of their character"

**8**

2,500-gallon water-storage tank trucks fed 21 portable water fountains

Legend has it one man roller-skated over 700 miles from Chicago to get to the march, while an 82-year-old cycled from Ohio

Volunteers prepared **80,000** packed lunches, each including a cheese sandwich, a slice of poundcake and an apple

## DID YOU KNOW?

In 1999, a group of 137 experts voted Martin's "I Have a Dream" speech the greatest of the 20th century

The "Big Six" leaders of the march, including Martin, met with President John F Kennedy in the Oval Office at the White House after the march was over

The following year President Lyndon B Johnson signed the Civil Rights Act, ending segregation in public places and banning job discrimination

# THE KING'S SPEECH

Martin was an outstanding public speaker – his "I Have a Dream" address changed the way people thought about race in America and has gone down in history as one of the greatest speeches ever given. More incredible still is that the words "I have a dream" weren't even in the notes he had in front of him – he added them on the day. Here are some of the other reasons his speech was so good…

> Fear of public speaking is called **GLOSSOPHOBIA** and it's very common - experts think up to 75% of the population worries about speaking in public to some degree

## M

### METAPHOR

This describes a situation by comparing it to other things, and Martin was an expert at it. There's a metaphor in every section and almost every paragraph of **"I Have a Dream"**.

Martin describes the end of slavery as a **"joyous daybreak to end the long night of captivity"** for black Americans. Discrimination in Mississippi is **"the heat of oppression"**, while racism is **"jangling"** across America, a word that makes the audience think of clinking jail keys

## A

### ALLUSION

This is when you refer to something that is supposed to make people think of a particular thing.

At the start of **"I Have a Dream"** Martin used the same kind of language that Abraham Lincoln (whose statue was behind him) had used when he spoke about abolishing slavery. This reminded the audience that it had been 100 years since promises of equality were first made. He also used quotes from the Bible, making his words sound holy and righteous

## R

### REPETITION

Using the same words again and again can reinforce a message and make the words feel poetic.

Talking about slavery at the start of the speech Martin repeats the phrase **"100 years later"** to remind the audience how long they have been waiting.

As the speech reaches its peak he uses the words **"I have a dream…"** nine times in a row – each time giving people a vision of a better future.

He then switches to the phrase **"let freedom ring"** – using it another 11 times

At the end of Martin's speech, a young man named George Raveling approached him and asked if he could have Martin's speech notes. Martin passed the three typewritten pages to George who, despite being offered **$3 million,** still refuses to sell them

**17** minutes
**How long the speech lasted**

# T

## TIMING

**"I Have a Dream"** starts slowly, but gradually gathers speed, like a song that reaches a climax.

At the beginning Martin speaks at only 80 words a minute (most people talk at around 120 words a minute). But as he gathers pace, he ends up speaking at 150 words a minute

**150** wpm

**120** wpm

**80** wpm

**START**

**FINISH**

**NORMAL SPEECH**

# I

## IMPROVISATION

During "**I Have a Dream**" Martin had been sticking to his script when gospel singer Mahalia Jackson shouted: **"Tell 'em about the dream, Martin!"** At that point he pushed his notes aside and began to freestyle. As a preacher, Martin was used to speaking in front of a crowd and like all great orators he adapted what he was saying to suit the mood of his audience

# N

## NOW

**"I Have a Dream"** was a call to action – what's the point of a speech if it isn't to inspire people to do something? The audience could feel Martin's sense of urgency throughout: **"We have... come to this hallowed spot to remind America of the fierce urgency of now. It would be fatal for the nation to overlook the urgency of the moment"**

# PUBLIC ENEMY №1

The FBI, NSA and CIA all spied on Martin in the 1950s and 60s. They feared he was a Communist and tried to give him a bad name by revealing secrets about his private life.

## THE FEDERAL BUREAU OF INVESTIGATION

called Martin **"the most dangerous man in America"**. Its leader, J Edgar Hoover, believed Martin was a Communist because he had a friend who was known to be a member of the Communist Party. The FBI had Martin put under surveillance and his phones were tapped right up until his death.

| NAME: | Martin Luther King Jr |
| --- | --- |
| NATIONALITY: | American |
| CITIZEN: | Yes |
| GENDER: | Male |
| RACE/ETHNICITY: | Black American |
| HEIGHT: | 1.69m |
| EYE COLOUR: | Brown |
| HAIR COLOUR: | Brown |
| DOB: | 15 January, 1929 |

## THE NATIONAL SECURITY AGENCY

also monitored Martin's phones as part of an operation to spy on famous Americans who opposed the war in Vietnam. Details of the operation, which also targeted boxer Muhammad Ali, were revealed many years later and the NSA even admitted it was "disreputable if not outright illegal".

## THE CENTRAL INTELLIGENCE AGENCY

investigated Martin after he was reportedly invited to Russia, which was America's greatest enemy at the time. They intercepted letters belonging to Martin and other civil rights leaders.

In 1964 Martin gave a speech in Jackson, Mississippi, where he said he was "sick and tired of people saying this movement has been infiltrated by Communists... There are as many Communists in this freedom movement as there are Eskimos in Florida".

# THE COLD WAR

At the time that Martin was campaigning for civil rights, America was involved in the Cold War. This was a 40-year political conflict between the East and the West, both of which had different ideas about the way countries should be ruled and run. Eastern countries like Russia favoured Communism, while western countries like America preferred Capitalism.

### WHAT IS COMMUNISM?

The government and the state are more important than individuals and the government selects its own leaders. Businesses are owned by the state and the government shares its wealth with its citizens

### WHAT IS CAPITALISM?

People's rights are important and they choose the government by voting. People can have their own businesses and make their own money

- Communist and alliances
- Western Bloc and alliances
- Unaligned

# ASSASSINATED!

On 3 April, 1968, Martin travelled to Memphis to organise a march in support of black sanitation workers (rubbish collectors) who were striking over poor working conditions and unfair pay. He checked into the Lorraine Motel where he'd stayed a number of times before.

## LORRAINE MOTEL

At 6:01pm on 4 April, Martin was standing on the second floor balcony outside room 306 when he was shot by a sniper's bullet. Doctors tried to save him but he died an hour later at a nearby hospital.

**LINE OF FIRE: 62.5M**

## BOARDING HOUSE

Shortly after the shot was fired, witnesses saw a man running away from the boarding house. Inside a shared upstairs bathroom police found a bullet cartridge, the window screen pushed out and scuff marks in the tub under the window. A man had checked in that afternoon under the name John Willard.

## CANIPE AMUSEMENT CO

Minutes later a bundle was found outside Canipe Amusement store containing a rifle, a pair of binoculars and some other belongings. Police learned that the rifle had been purchased five days before in Birmingham, Alabama by someone named Harvey Lowmayer.

## JAILED

Ray was flown back to America where he was charged with Martin's murder. He pleaded guilty in March of the following year – which spared him the death penalty – and he was sentenced to 99 years in prison. He died in jail in 1998.

## ON THE RUN

Ray fled to Atlanta in his Ford Mustang, where he ditched the car and took a bus to Detroit. From there he travelled by taxi across the border into Canada. After hiding out for a month, he acquired a Canadian passport under the name Ramon George Sneyd and caught a flight to England. On 8 June, 1968, two months after Martin's death, Ray was arrested at London Heathrow Airport trying to leave the UK for Brussels.

## MAN HUNT

Forensic detectives found fingerprints in the boarding house that the FBI matched to James Earl Ray. When they compared Ray's photo to the photo of Eric S Galt, they realised it was the same person. The FBI launched a man hunt.

### DID YOU KNOW?

Although James Earl Ray admitted killing Martin, he later claimed he was innocent and spent much of the rest of his life trying to clear his name

## WHITE FORD MUSTANG

Police found clothing in the boarding house with tags on from a laundry service in Los Angeles. The laundry service's records came up with the name Eric S Galt. Then when police ran a check on a white Ford Mustang that was found abandoned in a parking lot in Atlanta, it came back as registered to an Eric S Galt, and the FBI managed to find a photo of him.

WANTED BY THE FBI

CIVIL RIGHTS - CONSPIRACY
INTERSTATE FLIGHT - ROBBERY
JAMES EARL RAY

FBI No. 405,942 G

Photographs taken 1960

Photograph taken 1968 (eyes drawn by artist)

ses: Eric Starvo Galt, W. C. Herron, Harvey Lowmyer, James McBride, James O'Conner, James Walton, James Walyon, John Willard, "Jim,"

**DESCRIPTION**

Age: 40, born March 10, 1928, at Quincy or Alton, Illinois (not supported by birth records)
Height: 5' 10"
Weight: 163 to 174 pounds
Build: Medium
Hair: Brown, possibly cut short
Eyes: Blue
Complexion: Medium
Race: White
Nationality: American
Occupations: Baker, color matcher, laborer
Scars and Marks: Small scar on center of forehead and small scar on palm of right hand
My protruding left ear; reportedly is a lone wolf; allegedly attended dance instruction
...pleted course in bartending.

NW 9 U 000 12

# FINAL FRONTIER

In 1967 Martin met black actress Nichelle Nichols, who played the role of Lieutenant Uhura in the legendary TV show *Star Trek*. Nichelle was thinking of leaving television and going to act in the theatre, but Martin told her that he was a "Trekkie" and that *Star Trek* was the only programme he allowed his children to watch. He said she was one of the few black Americans playing a main character on TV and, even more importantly, she was playing someone who was seen as intelligent and equal to those around her – something that was very rare for black people at that time. Nichelle suddenly realised how powerful her role was, and decided to stay.

Director Gene Roddenberry deliberately included actors from different cultural backgrounds in the first *Star Trek* crew, because he wanted to show an ideal future

DID YOU KNOW ?

When black actress Whoopi Goldberg first saw the character of Uhura on TV, she cried, "Momma! There's a black lady on TV, and she ain't no maid!" Whoopi became a huge *Star Trek* fan and asked to be given a role on *Star Trek: The Next Generation*

In 1968 *Star Trek* showed the first ever inter-racial kiss on American TV, between Captain Kirk and Lieutenant Uhura

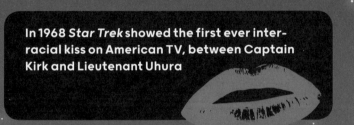

## WHY WAS UHURA'S ROLE IMPORTANT?

When you see someone like yourself in a positive role it can make you feel accepted, inspired and self-confident.

When you see someone who looks different to you in a positive role it can make you feel interested, respectful and compassionate

Recent Marvel superhero movie *Black Panther* also shows black people in a strong light, as rulers, royalty and creators of advanced technology

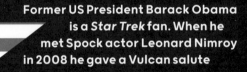

Former US President Barack Obama is a *Star Trek* fan. When he met Spock actor Leonard Nimroy in 2008 he gave a Vulcan salute

Astronaut Ronald McNair, the second black person in space, was inspired to become an astronaut because of the character of Uhura. Ronald's brother said,

"*Star Trek* showed the future where there were black folk and white folk working together"

*Star Trek* fans are called "Trekkies" and are the only fans to be included by name in the Oxford English Dictionary

ENGLISH DICTIONARY

# WE SHALL OVERCOME

Martin's actions changed America. Black Americans could now vote freely. They could choose where they sat on buses and eat their lunch at any counter. But there was another problem: poverty. Black Americans were less likely to have good jobs, which meant they earned less money, had fewer opportunities and were more likely to become involved in crime. And sadly the same is still true today. Martin's peaceful protests solved many of the problems, but his work isn't finished. Passionate people continue to fight for the rights of all Americans. Martin's dream of a fair and just society where everyone is treated equally lives on.

Becomes legal for black and white Americans to marry **1967**

Voting Rights Act says black Americans can't be stopped from voting in elections **1965**

Martin wins Nobel Peace Prize

Civil Rights Act bans segregation in public places and job discrimination

Time magazine names Martin "Man of the Year" for 1963 **1964**

FEBRUARY 18, 1957

TWENTY CENTS

# TIME
### THE WEEKLY NEWSMAGAZINE

Montgomery, Alabama's
REV. MARTIN LUTHER KING

**1968** Fair Housing Act makes it illegal to discriminate against non-whites when buying or renting property

**1986** First Martin Luther King Jr Day, some states refuse to observe it

Oprah Winfrey launches talk show

**1995** Million Man March is largest black demonstration in history

**2000** All 50 states observe Martin Luther King Jr Day for first time

**2001** Colin Powell is America's first black Secretary of State

**2008** Barack Obama is first black President of the United States

**2011** Martin Luther King Jr memorial opens in Washington DC

**2013** Black Lives Matter movement is founded

**2016** National Museum of African American History and Culture opens

DR. MARTIN LUTHER KING JR. BOULEVARD

# GLOSSARY

**EQUAL RIGHTS NOW**

**WE DEMAND AN END TO BIAS**

### ACT
A law passed by the government

### ACTIVIST
A person who takes action against something they feel is wrong

### ASSASSINATION
The murder of an important person

### BAPTIST
A member of a Baptist church. Baptists share many beliefs with other Christians, but place particular importance on baptism (immersing people in water)

### BOYCOTT
To stop using or buying something as a way to protest against it

### CIVIL RIGHTS
The rights that everyone has to freedom and equality

### COMMUNIST
A person who believes that the government should own everything and share it between its citizens

### DISCRIMINATION
The unfair treatment of a person or group of people, usually because of their gender, religion or race

### JIM CROW LAWS
Unfair rules that discriminated against black Americans

### MINISTER
A clergyman of the church

### NOBEL PEACE PRIZE
One of the most admired awards in the world, given to someone who has worked to encourage peace

### PREACHER
A person who gives talks on religion, such as a minister

### PROHIBITED
Not allowed by law

### SEGREGATION
Keeping a person or group of people separate from the rest of society

### SERMON
A speech, usually given in church

### SIT-IN
A type of protest in which people sit in one place and refuse to leave

### STRIKE
When workers refuse to work to force an employer to agree to their demands

### SUPREME COURT
The highest court in the United States of America

Button BOOKS

First published 2020 by Button Books, an imprint of Guild of Master Craftsman Publications Ltd, Castle Place, 166 High Street, Lewes, East Sussex, BN7 1XU, UK. Copyright in the Work © GMC Publications Ltd, 2020. ISBN 978 1 78708 056 0. Distributed by Publishers Group West in the United States. All rights reserved. No part of this publication may be reproduced, stored in a retrieval system or transmitted in any form or by any means without the prior permission of the publisher and copyright owner. While every effort has been made to obtain permission from the copyright holders for all material used in this book, the publishers will be pleased to hear from anyone who has not been appropriately acknowledged and to make the correction in future reprints. The publishers and authors can accept no legal responsibility for any consequences arising from the application of information, advice or instructions given in this publication. A catalogue record for this book is available from the British Library. Senior Project Editor: Susie Duff. Design: Matt Carr, Jo Chapman. Illustrations: Alex Bailey, Matt Carr, Shutterstock. Colour origination by GMC Reprographics. Printed and bound in China.